Inside
Government

☆ CONSTITUTIONAL ☆
AMENDMENTS

Barbara Silberdick Feinberg

Twenty-First Century Books

A Division of Henry Holt and Company

New York

Twenty-First Century Books
A Division of Henry Holt and Company, Inc.
115 West 18th Street
New York, NY 10011

Henry Holt® and colophon are trademarks of
Henry Holt and Company, Inc.
Publishers since 1866

Published in Canada by Fitzhenry & Whiteside Ltd.
195 Allstate Parkway, Markham, Ontario L3R 4T8

Library of Congress Cataloging-in-Publication Data
Feinberg, Barbara Silberdick.
Constitutional amendments / Barbara Silberdick Feinberg.
p.   cm.—(Inside government)
Includes bibliographical references and index.
Summary: Examines the twenty-seven amendments that have been
adopted since the Constitution was approved more than 200 years ago.
1. United States—Constitution—Amendments—Juvenile literature.
2. United States—Constitutional law—Amendments—Juvenile literature.
3. United States—Constitutional history—Juvenile literature. [1. United States—
Constitution—Amendments. 2. United States—Constitutional law—Amendments.
3. United States—Constitutional history.] I. Title II. Series.
KF4555.Z9F45   1996
342.73'03–dc20   96-16235
[347.3023]   CIP
                                                                        AC
ISBN 0-8050-4619-4
First Edition—1996

Designed by Kelly Soong

Printed in Mexico
All first editions are printed on acid-free paper. ∞
1 3 5 7 9 10 8 6 4 2

Photo credits

pp. 10, 29, 58: The Granger Collection; pp. 16, 61: Brown Brothers; p. 38: Corbis-Bettmann;
pp. 41, 46: UPI/Corbis-Bettmann; p. 51: Stock Montage, Inc.; p. 69: Sylvia Johnson/Woodfin
Camp & Associates, Inc.

☆

In memory of my aunt, Clarice Katz Silverdick

☆ ══════ **ACKNOWLEDGMENTS** ══════ ☆

I would like to thank the following people for helping me to locate some of the background information used in this book or for discussing constitutional problems with me: Floyd Abrams, attorney, Cahill Gordon, and Reindel; Irving Adelman, Assistant Director, Head of Reference, East Meadow Public Library in East Meadow, New York; Marilyn Bunshaft, Community Affairs Officer, East Meadow Public Library; Michael Neft, New York University School of Law, Class of 1996; and Professor Steven McSloy, New York University School of Law.

CONTENTS

ONE
MAKING CHANGES IN THE CONSTITUTION

A CONSTITUTION TO REPLACE THE ARTICLES OF CONFEDERATION: AN OVERVIEW

In May 1787, fifty-five men met in Philadelphia to find remedies for the defective Articles of Confederation. Adopted in 1781, the Articles created a league of independent states whose members were the thirteen former British colonies. It also established an ineffective central government that had no direct control over the people and only enough power to carry out the states' wishes. The Confederation was so weak that it had been unable to stop trade wars among its members, raise enough money to meet its expenses and repay foreign loans, or open foreign-controlled ports in North America to American ships. In 1786, it could not even raise an army to put down a debtors' rebellion in Massachusetts led by Captain Daniel Shays. (Eventually the state militia restored order.) Many leaders of the War of Independence were fearful that the fragile Confederation might dissolve. They had called the meeting in Philadelphia to discuss ways to strengthen and improve the Articles.

The agreement of all thirteen member states was needed to pass formal changes, called amendments, to the Articles. Since the state of Rhode Island did not send delegates to the meeting, under the rigid unanimity rule the Articles could not be altered or rewritten. Some delegates in Philadelphia were then ready to replace the Articles: it would be easier to scrap the Confederation than to fix it. By the end of May, the delegates began to discuss a plan for a new national government—the Virginia Plan, prepared by James Madison and presented by Governor Edmund Randolph. Soon other plans were offered, and many compromises were negotiated.

Some three months later, the delegates produced a 4,300-word document known as the Constitution to correct the defects of the Articles of Confederation. It set up a national government, defined and limited its powers, and outlined its relations with the states. The Confederation's central government contained only a single-house legislature of delegates from member states. The new national government, however, was divided into three parts, each with specific duties: a legislature, called the Congress, to make laws; an executive, led by a president, to carry them out; and a judiciary, or court system, to decide disputes over laws and to judge those who break the laws. The Congress itself had two houses: the Senate, which represented the states equally, and the House of Representatives, which determined representation by the population of each state. The Constitution also transformed relations between the government and the states. The new government now shared power over the people with the states, and if its laws conflicted with state laws, national laws would be supreme.

THE FRAMERS' PROPOSALS
FOR AMENDING THE CONSTITUTION

The framers wanted their Constitution to be more flexible than the Articles of Confederation. Knowing that times and circumstances would change, they searched for a way the Constitution could be altered without requiring the consent of all the states. As early as June 11, 1787, George Mason, a delegate from Virginia, explained why this was important:

> The plan now to be formed will certainly be defective, as the Confederation has been found on trial to be. Amendments

therefore will be necessary, and it will be better to provide for them, in an easy, regular, and Constitutional way than to trust to chance and violence.

The Virginia Plan called for amendments but offered few details. It did, however, specifically exclude Congress from the amending process, to protect the states from government interference in their internal matters. Also, its authors doubted that the government would voluntarily correct its own abuses of power.

The issue of amendments was postponed and referred to the Committee of Detail, which worked on the first draft of the Constitution from July 26 to August 6. A member of the committee, James Wilson of Pennsylvania, suggested that Congress call a special convention to consider amendments upon the request of two-thirds of the state legislatures. Wilson's proposal resembled arrangements in the constitutions of Pennsylvania (1776), Georgia (1776), Vermont (1777), Massachusetts (1780), and New Hampshire (1784), which provided that changes be made by specially selected conventions of delegates in order to distinguish between amendment drafting and ordinary lawmaking. Wilson's scheme was approved by the delegates on August 30, 1787.

The framers did not debate the issue of amendments until September, when their meeting was drawing to a close. Other sections of the Constitution had received far more attention. On September 10, Elbridge Gerry of Massachusetts asked that the amendments clause be reexamined. He was unhappy with the Constitution because he felt that the national government was now too powerful. He objected that national conventions called to draft amendments might eventually undermine, and then eliminate, state constitutions.

Alexander Hamilton of New York objected to the amendments clause for different reasons. First, he felt that it did not let the people participate in the amending process. He proposed that the Congress, representing the people, should also be

☆ ═══════ ☆

George Washington presided at the
Constitutional Convention at Philadelphia in 1787.

allowed to call for an amendments convention by a two-thirds vote. He wanted "an easy mode . . . for supplying defects which will probably appear in the new System." Secondly, he worried that the states might use a national convention to unravel the Constitution. Adapting a proposal offered by Roger Sherman of Connecticut, Hamilton, joined by Madison, suggested that Congress propose changes that would go into effect if state legislatures or state conventions approved them. John Rutledge of South Carolina, fearing that such a procedure would allow the national government to tamper with slavery, succeeded in adding a sentence that thereby protected the slave trade from government interference until 1808. The amendments clause was then sent to the Committee on Style, to be written into the final draft of the Constitution. It was ready to be sent to the states on September 17.

On September 15, the delegates again debated the amendments clause. Sherman and delegates from other small states wanted to add a provision to protect the states' control over their internal matters and their equality of representation in the Senate. Madison objected: "Begin with these special provisions, and every State will insist on them. . . ." Gerry and Gouverneur Morris of Pennsylvania were still reluctant to give the national government so much power over the states. They wanted Congress to call for a national amending convention if two-thirds of the states requested it.

After much heated discussion, the final version of Article 5, on amendments, was added to the Constitution. The measure included a number of compromises: it protected the slave trade until 1808, an important issue for Southern states, and prevented changes to deny equal representation of the states in the Senate, a matter of concern to small states. It also gave both Congress and the states the opportunity to propose amendments. This satisfied those who feared that states would undo the Constitution, as well as those who doubted that the national legislature would correct its own abuse of power.

HOW THE CONSTITUTION IS AMENDED

Article 5 states that amendments can be proposed by a two-thirds vote in both houses of Congress or by a convention called at the demand of two-thirds of the states. Ratification, or approval, requires the consent of three-fourths of the state legislatures or the consent of conventions in three-fourths of the states, whichever of these methods Congress suggests. The requirements are easier than the Articles, but difficult enough to discourage frequent use. Presently, 290 members of the House of Representatives and sixty-seven senators must agree to propose an amendment. The consent of thirty-eight states is required for ratification.

Article 5 did not set time limits for ratification. The Twenty-sixth Amendment, granting voting rights to eighteen-, nineteen-, and twenty-year-olds, was the quickest to win approval, taking only three months. On the other hand, the Twenty-seventh Amendment, requiring an election to take place before congressional pay increases could take effect, was the longest, taking 203 years. Congress did not add deadlines to the first seventeen amendments to the Constitution, all of which were adopted within seven years of proposal. Then in 1917, for the first time, the lawmakers attached a seven-year deadline to an amendment. This was the Eighteenth Amendment, which outlawed the sale and manufacture of alcoholic beverages. In *Dillon v. Gloss*, decided in 1921, the Supreme Court, the nation's highest court, ruled that a seven-year time limit was permissible according to the Constitution. Since then, all amendments have contained that deadline. In 1979, after the Equal Rights Amendment for women failed to win enough states to be ratified, Congress extended the deadline by three years. That extension expired before the Supreme Court could decide whether or not it violated the Constitution.

Article 5 did not say whether states could rescind, or take back, their ratifications. It also failed to note whether states could reject amendments and then reverse their decisions. In 1939, the Supreme Court heard *Coleman v. Miller*, a case that questioned a state's right to ratify an amendment after having previously rejected it twelve years earlier. (The proposed amendment, which failed, would have banned child labor.) The Court held that issues relating to the ratification of amendments are best decided by Congress. Currently, a state may change its decision and approve an amendment it earlier rejected. Congress, however, will not accept a state's reversing a ratification.

Once an amendment wins approval, Congress is usually notified and given some time to review the ratification documents. Then the amendment must be certified in order to take effect. This means that certificates of ratification from the states are checked to ensure they meet the terms of Article 5 and that they have all used the same words. Finally, the amendment is printed in the *Federal Register*, the official listing of all government laws and rules. From 1791 until 1951, the Secretary of State was responsible for certifying amendments; Congress then gave the job to the Administrator of General Services, an official who oversees the publication of the *Federal Register*. In 1984, Congress transferred certification to the Archivist of the United States, who preserves important national documents.

Only twenty-seven amendments have been adopted since the Constitution was approved more than two hundred years ago. They have helped to make an eighteenth-century document serve the needs of nineteenth- and twentieth-century Americans. Among the amendments that have been ratified and certified are the ten that make up the Bill of Rights, which protects citizens' freedoms. Other amendments made citizenship and voting rights available to more Americans. The remainder made adjustments in procedures and activities affecting the president, the courts, and Congress.

TWO
ADDING A
BILL OF RIGHTS

DEMANDS FOR A BILL OF RIGHTS

The Articles of Confederation did not contain a bill of rights. Since the central government had no direct power over the people, no safeguards for their freedom were thought necessary. Besides, citizens' liberties were protected by state constitutions. At the Constitutional Convention in Philadelphia in August 1787, some of the delegates, including George Mason of Virginia, Charles Pinckney of South Carolina, James McHenry of Maryland, and Elbridge Gerry of Massachusetts, worried that the new national government would be too powerful. These delegates offered piecemeal changes to the Constitution that would protect personal liberty. Among the changes that were accepted were prohibitions against bills of attainder, which were legislative acts that punished specific individuals without benefit of a trial, and ex post facto laws, which imposed penalties for actions that were not crimes when the actions took place.

In September, during the last week of the convention, Mason, the principal author of the 1776 Virginia Declaration of Rights, suggested that a bill of rights be added to the Constitution to "give great quiet to the people." Roger Sherman of Connecticut disagreed, remarking that state bills of rights "are not repealed by this Constitution." Most of the delegates sided with Sherman when the matter came to a vote. Throughout their stay in Philadelphia, the weather had been very hot—the delegates were tired and uncomfortable. After working on the Constitution for four months, they were eager to get home.

In England, American minister John Adams received news of the Constitution from Gerry. While pleased with most of the document, Adams wrote to fellow diplomat Thomas Jefferson, who was in Paris, "What do you think of a Declaration of Rights? Should not such a Thing have preceded the Model?" Jefferson also received a letter from James Madison, one of the main authors of the Constitution, containing his views on the document. Madison opposed a bill of rights. He felt that personal freedoms were adequately protected under state constitutions. In his reply to Madison, Jefferson listed the items in the new Constitution that he liked. Then he wrote, "I will now add what I do not like, first the omission of a bill of rights." He returned to the subject at the end of his letter: "Let me add that a bill of rights is what the people are entitled to against every government on earth, general or particular, & what no just government should refuse, or rest on inference."

In each of the states, opponents of the Constitution, known as the Anti-Federalists, tried to block its ratification. Among their objections to the document was the absence of a bill of rights. The writings of Anti-Federalists Mason, Richard Henry Lee of Virginia, and George Clinton of New York received the widest circulation. Supporters of the Constitution, called Federalists, included John Jay and Alexander Hamilton of New York, and James Madison of Virginia. They prepared a series of essays defending the new plan of government, which also reached a large audience.

At first, the success of the Constitution seemed assured as states began to approve it by landslide votes. Acceptance by nine states was needed for it to go into effect, however, and the ratifying conventions in Massachusetts, New York, and Virginia were divided. Anti-Federalists threatened to call for a second convention to make improvements to the Constitution. Federalists feared that another convention would severely weaken the

*An interesting composite shows many of the delegates to
the First Congress under the Constitution in 1789.*

new government. The two sides struck a compromise: the Anti-Federalists consented to the Constitution, and the Federalists promised to add a bill of rights.

In the First Congress, Madison was determined to carry out the Federalist pledge. His opposition to a bill of rights had almost cost him a seat in the legislature. Anti-Federalist Patrick Henry, a patriot and former governor of Virginia, led the fight to keep Madison out of the Senate. Madison later barely defeated Anti-Federalist James Monroe, a future president, in an election to the House of Representatives. After losing the Senate seat, Madison changed his mind about a bill of rights. In a letter to Jefferson, he explained that, on the one hand, a bill of rights would do little to check the real threat to personal liberty—the ill-informed, intolerant opinions of the majority of citizens. On the other hand, he would accept it as a means of educating the public and possibly protecting individuals from arbitrary actions by the government.

DRAWING UP A BILL OF RIGHTS

Once in Congress, Madison worked hard to reduce to a reasonable list the more than two hundred proposed amendments drawn from state ratifying conventions. On May 4, 1789, and then again on May 25, two months after the First Congress assembled, he announced his intention to introduce a bill of rights. A number of lawmakers objected that time was needed to organize the government before Congress started to change the Constitution. Madison urged them to take action so "that our constituents [the people Congress represents] may see that we pay a proper attention to a subject they have much at heart." On June 8, he was finally able to present the first amendments to Congress. After a delay, the House debated them in mid-August. Madison wanted the amendments to be added into the appropriate paragraphs of the Constitution. Roger Sherman of Connecticut, however, convinced the representatives that the amendments should be kept separate. He argued that the Constitution was already accepted by the people through their states. The amendments would be approved as acts of the state governments.

On August 24, seventeen draft amendments were sent to the Senate, whose proceedings at that time were held in secret. The Senate reduced the amendments to twelve. Then a conference committee of senators and representatives negotiated the differences. The House approved the final list on September 24, and the Senate followed with two votes on September 25 and 26. (It is unclear why the second Senate vote took place.) Within two years, nine states ratified ten of the amendments, but since Vermont had entered the Union on March 4, 1791, approval by one more state was needed. Virginia supplied it on December 15. Two amendments failed to be ratified. A proposal to limit the number of people represented by each lawmaker to thirty thousand. (It would have created an unwieldy House of Representatives today.) The other proposal affecting pay increases for lawmakers would be accepted two centuries later. On March 1, 1792, Secretary of State Thomas Jefferson certified that the ten amendments, otherwise known as the Bill of Rights, were part of the Constitution.

Originally, the ten amendments applied only to the national government. During the twentieth century, the Supreme Court gradually began to extend them to the actions of state governments as well. Most Americans today know what the Bill of Rights is, but how many citizens can describe all ten amendments?

A DESCRIPTION OF THE BILL OF RIGHTS

The **FIRST AMENDMENT** is a statement of eighteenth-century notions of basic human rights. It focuses on political and civil freedoms but is silent on the subject of economic and social rights—matters of additional concern to the twentieth century. Nevertheless, it is the most famous amendment to the Constitution.

The Church of England, supported by the state, imposed severe penalties on those who refused to accept its beliefs or pay for its upkeep. Puritans, Quakers, Baptists, and Roman Catholics, among others, colonized North America to escape being punished for their beliefs. At first, the colonies were intolerant of those who did not accept their religious doctrines. Anne Hutchinson was banished in 1637 because she disagreed with the ministers of the Massachusetts Bay Colony. As late as 1776, many colonies still required religious tests as a condition of holding public office. Lawmakers in Georgia, for example, had to be "of the Protestant religion."

Because so many religious sects had come to the colonies, tolerance and the separation of church and state gradually gained acceptance. Roger Williams left the Massachusetts Bay Colony in 1636 to establish a settlement in Rhode Island that would allow freedom of worship. In 1752, many New Yorkers refused to support a Church of England college with their taxes. In 1759, East Apthorp led a Church of England mission to convert Massachusetts dissenters. He attacked their beliefs mercilessly. His outbursts led citizens to the fear that Parliament, the British legislature, would impose the English religion on them as well as deprive them of their liberties as citizens. After the War of Independence, state constitutions began to contain guarantees of freedom of religion. A notable example was Jefferson's statute on religious tolerance, passed in 1786, which separated church and state and guaranteed freedom of belief.

In neither Britain nor the colonies did the principle of free speech necessarily protect those who criticized the government. Freedom of expression meant licenses to permit publication and the absence of prior censorship. It did not, however, protect writers or printers from prosecution after a speech was given or a pamphlet was published. That would await the future. John Peter Zenger was one of the few who escaped punishment for criticizing the government. He had printed articles mocking William Cosby, the governor of New York. Zenger was tried in 1735 but was acquitted because what he had printed about the governor was true—at that time a novel defense. When Parliament passed the Stamp Act in 1765, taxing all printed matter, and the Intolerable Acts of 1774, closing the port of Boston and bringing the colonial government under direct British control, Sam Adams and other agitators spoke out in protest. As a result, Adams had to hide from the authorities. Under British law, people could write or say what they thought, in public, but they risked punishment afterward. In 1776, even Thomas Jefferson helped draft a law to penalize those who spoke out in support of the British. Criticism of the government or its policies—at least during wartime—remained a crime into the twentieth century.

The right to meet in groups and join clubs is part of the First Amendment.

When John Adams drafted the Massachusetts bill of rights, he included freedom of assembly. Citizens in Massachusetts remembered that under the Intolerable Acts, their town meetings could not be held without the royal governor's permission; they also needed his approval of the topics they wanted to discuss. The New Hampshire constitution also mentioned this right of assembly, but most other state constitutions did not.

Freedom to petition the government to have wrongs righted is also found in the First Amendment.

The British Bill of Rights, passed by Parliament in 1689, included the freedom to petition the government. In the 1760s and 1770s, however, King George III and his ministers ignored the colonists' many petitions protesting government policies and their loss of rights. This is why freedom to petition the government was repeated in numerous bills of rights attached to state constitutions in the 1770s and 1780s.

The **Second Amendment** protects the right to bear arms, to own guns.

The right to bear arms is linked to the need for states to be able to raise militias to maintain their own security. The amendment reflects the former colonists' and their British ancestors' fears that a powerful central government could maintain a standing army in peacetime and use it to tyrannize them. After all, British troops had been stationed in the colonies. The troops' unpopularity led to the Boston Massacre, where the troops fired on people who had thrown snowballs and jeered at them. Also, rifles were essential in the colonies for hunting food and protecting homes from attacks by hostile Indians.

The **Third Amendment** prohibits the government from forcing people to lodge soldiers in their homes in peacetime, and to do so only as laws might require during wartime.

Prior to the War of Independence, Americans had been made to feed and house British soldiers to offset the cost of their upkeep in the colonies. The colonists fiercely resented this government policy.

According to the **FOURTH AMENDMENT**, federal law-enforcement officials may not arrest people or search their homes without a specific search warrant. The warrant must describe the location to be searched and/or the items to be removed. There must be a good reason to intrude on people's privacy.

The Fourth amendment was the result of the colonists' outrage over writs of assistance, general search warrants issued by Parliament. These writs allowed British customs officers to search homes and businesses, whenever they chose, wherever they chose, without any limits. In 1761, James Otis, a Boston lawyer, argued that writs of assistance violated British legal tradition; he lost the case. In 1772, abuse of these writs was one of the reasons Bostonians drew up "A List of Infringements and Violations of Those Rights." They protested that "our houses and even our bed chambers are exposed to be ransacked, our boxes, our chests, and trunks broke open, ravaged and plundered by wretches, whom no prudent man would venture to employ even as menial servants."

The **FIFTH AMENDMENT** safeguards the rights of people accused of serious crimes that may involve the death penalty.

The origins of the Fifth Amendment can be traced to the Magna Carta of 1215, the first written statement of the rights of Englishmen; the Petition of Right of 1628, which restrained King Charles I's abuse of power over his subjects; and the Bill of Rights of 1689, a reaction to King James II's headstrong rule. These documents restated the freedoms that British citizens traditionally enjoyed and placed restraints on their rulers.

Before civilians may be brought to trial, they must be indicted, or accused, by a grand jury, the group of twelve to twenty-three people who decide whether there is enough evidence to bring formal charges of a crime against the accused.

Americans were familiar with the British common law requirement of indictment. (Common law developed from local customs and judges' decisions rather than by acts of Parliament.) American colonists were also acquainted with the writings of Sir Edward Coke and Sir William Blackstone (published in the colonies in 1772) on common law.

No one may be tried twice for the same crime.

Another principle of British common law protects individuals from double jeopardy. It does not, however, prevent them from facing separate federal and state prosecutions for the same crime or from appealing unfavorable verdicts. It also does not prevent them from being retried if a jury cannot reach a verdict.

People cannot be made to testify against themselves.

The safeguard against self-incrimination can be traced to the 1637 trial in Britain of Puritan agitator John Lilburne. Taken before the Star Chamber, a royal court noted for its arbitrary methods and severe punishments, Lilburne had protested his questioning by the councillors who made up the court: "I am not willing to answer to you any more of these questions, because I see you go about by this Examination to ensnare me." For his refusal to testify against himself, Lilburne was whipped, fined, and placed in solitary confinement. He was released in 1641, the year Parliament abolished the Star Chamber.

Proper and fair legal procedures must be followed before people accused of major crimes can be compelled to lose their lives, freedom, or property.

The requirement known as due process of law is another right inherited from Britain. Church courts used to try people for heresy, or "incorrect beliefs," and often extracted answers by torture. Later, the courts required people to swear to tell the truth without informing them of the crime they were accused of committing. They could be punished for failing to so swear, or for giving truthful answers that proved they committed a crime, even though they did not know the nature of the charges against them. Or, they could lie and be convicted of perjury, the failure to tell the truth under oath.

The government must pay property owners a fair price when it seizes their land for a public use, such as highway construction.

Parliament and colonial governments often confiscated private property for public projects—a process known as eminent domain. Owners were compelled to turn over their land, but they were not always paid, or paid enough, a problem remedied by the Fifth Amendment.

According to the **SIXTH AMENDMENT**, people accused of crimes deserve a speedy, public trial by jury, conducted in the area where they live. They have the right to be told the nature of the charges against them, to confront witnesses who testify against them, to compel witnesses to testify for them, and to be provided with a lawyer if they cannot afford one.

Most of these Sixth Amendment rights can be traced to twelfth-century England, but they did not necessarily protect American colonists. For example, colonists were sometimes tried in British Admiralty courts, which handled cases related to shipping and other naval matters. These courts did not offer jury trials or follow all traditional legal procedures. What's more, they were located far from the colonists' homes—for example, in Halifax, Nova Scotia—where local Canadian residents would be less sympathetic to the colonists' plight.

The **SEVENTH AMENDMENT** guarantees the right to a trial by jury for disputes involving more than $20.

The Seventh Amendment is another British common-law rule adopted by Americans. Most colonists preferred to be tried by juries in cases concerning monetary disputes because juries would be more incorruptible and impartial than British-appointed judges. Urging this amendment, as well as others, American judge Samuel Bryan, writing under the pen name Centinel, pointed out that without jury trials, British merchants would have a much better chance of collecting the pre-Revolutionary debts the Americans owed them. Today most people do not use federal courts unless larger amounts of money are at stake.

The **EIGHTH AMENDMENT** prohibits courts from setting excessive bail (the money deposited to ensure that a person accused of a crime will show up for trial) and excessive fines (money paid as a penalty for a crime). It also bans the use of cruel and unusual punishments.

Concern with high bail and excessive fines has its roots in thirteenth-century England, when court officers were first warned not to force prisoners to pay money in return for more lenient treatment. The 1689 British Bill of Rights outlawed cruel and unusual punishments, but defining such punishment was another matter. Blackstone, the famous British legal scholar, allowed a number of punishments that would torture or maim prisoners, including disemboweling and branding. Americans gradually adopted less gruesome methods.

The **NINTH AMENDMENT** assures Americans that they still have additional, unlisted rights. The Constitution and the Bill of Rights did not attempt to mention every basic human right.

Alexander Hamilton warned that amendments designed to protect specific rights could prove dangerous: later on, it might be thought that the people had surrendered any freedoms not itemized in a bill of rights. The Ninth Amendment was written to meet this objection by reserving these unwritten rights to the people.

The **TENTH AMENDMENT** gives to the state and to the people all those powers that are not granted to the national government or denied to the states.

James Wilson of Pennsylvania was one of the Federalists who did not think the Tenth Amendment was needed. He argued that the national government would have no powers other than those specifically listed in the Constitution. Fear of a central government was widespread, however. Most of the states demanded a guarantee that they would continue to control their own internal affairs. For this reason, the Tenth Amendment reserved those powers not mentioned in the Constitution to the states and the people. The Ninth and Tenth Amendments serve as reminders that the people are sovereign within their states.

☆　☆　☆

Ratified in 1791, the Bill of Rights did not extend to two important groups in the nation—blacks and women. In 1787, about 650,000 Africans were enslaved in the United States. As the price of union between Southern states and the rest of the nation, they received no protection from the Constitution. Thomas Jefferson could write that "the abolition of domestic slavery is the great object of desire," a view shared by Patrick Henry, but only Massachusetts declared slavery unenforceable within its borders, in 1783. The nation's 1.5 million women were also denied citizenship and treated as dependents. Abigail Adams asked her husband, John, for laws to curb the "unlimited power" of husbands over their wives, but her request was ignored. Much remained to be done to extend citizenship and voting rights to more Americans.

THREE
EXTENDING CITIZENSHIP AND VOTING RIGHTS

The denial of political and legal rights to blacks and women was acceptable to most eighteenth-century Americans. Young people were also treated as dependents. As teenagers, they were old enough to give their lives defending their country in wartime, but they were not allowed to vote in elections until they turned twenty-one, the legal age of consent. To remedy these injustices, seven amendments were added to the Constitution during the nineteenth and twentieth centuries. Collectively, they made more Americans full citizens of the United States by promising voting rights and equal treatment before the law.

RIGHTS FOR BLACKS

Five amendments were needed to help blacks gain the benefits of American citizenship; three were passed as a result of the Civil War (1861–1865). In 1863, more than three million black slaves lived in the Confederacy, the government formed by the eleven Southern states that left the Union. Another 450,000 slaves toiled in the four border states that did not secede, and some 500,000 free blacks were scattered throughout the nation. In the North, free blacks had limited rights to petition, travel, organize, and publish, but because of racial prejudice against them, most were not allowed to vote. Often, they held unskilled jobs. In the South, freed blacks had fewer rights but greater economic opportunities, as craftspeople and tradespersons.

The **THIRTEENTH AMENDMENT** frees slaves and guarantees that people cannot be forced to work against their will unless they are being punished for a crime. Congress has the right to pass laws to carry out this amendment.

Some citizens condemned slavery since the early days of the American republic. By the 1830s, abolitionist groups began their crusade to free slaves. They received a setback in the controversial Dred Scott case of 1857, in which the Supreme Court ruled that slaves were the property of their owners and were not citizens. Nevertheless, on his own, President Abraham Lincoln freed slaves living in the Confederacy with his 1863 Emancipation Proclamation. It was a war measure that would

☆ ══════ ☆

An American illustration of the time shows Roger Taney, chief justice of the U.S. Supreme Court, handing down his decision on the Dred Scott case.

probably expire when the conflict ended. An ordinary law passed by Congress wouldn't do because the Constitution recognized slavery. Article 1, Section 2 allowed the slave population to be counted as three-fifths of the white population for purposes of distributing seats in the House of Representatives and for determining taxes. To end slavery forever, the Constitution had to be changed, so the Thirteenth Amendment was proposed to the states.

Ratification presented a problem. Since the Union regarded the Confederacy as illegal, twenty-seven of the existing thirty-six states had to approve the new amendment for it to take effect. Eleven of those states were under military occupation and lacked civilian governments. After Kentucky and Delaware rejected the amendment, favorable votes in at least four former Confederate states were needed for ratification. Eight of the occupied Southern states were pressured to accept the amendment as a condition for reclaiming their seats in Congress. The amendment was added to the Constitution on December 6, 1865.

The Thirteenth Amendment was unique in several ways. It was the only amendment to the Constitution to be signed by the president of the United States. (Lincoln's motives were unclear, but he may have wanted simply to record his support for the official abolition of slavery.) It was also the first amendment to greatly expand the national government's powers by permitting Congress to interfere in the states' internal matters for purposes of enforcement.

The **FOURTEENTH AMENDMENT** is remembered for its broad definition of the rights of citizenship, which were officially granted to blacks as well as to qualified immigrants. In addition, the amendment contained harsh penalties for states that failed to comply with its requirements, but these penalties were never carried out.

In 1866, the Republicans in Congress created a Freedmen's Bureau to provide former slaves with welfare, relief, education, and employment. The lawmakers also passed the Civil Rights Act to define citizenship and safeguard civil rights. When Lincoln's successor, President Andrew Johnson, a Southerner, refused to sign these measures into law, Congress passed them a second time (as the Constitution requires) to override the president's decision. Eager to keep black rights from being further weakened by the president or struck down by the Supreme Court, Congressional Republicans decided to give blacks more lasting protection by adding the Fourteenth Amendment to the Constitution.

President Johnson's lenient treatment of the Southern states enabled many former Confederate officers to take control of state and local governments and to enact Black Codes, rules governing the conduct of newly freed slaves. In many states, jobless blacks could be arrested for loitering and "apprenticed" to whites. Laws establishing contracts between whites and their black servants often failed to protect the servants' rights. Blacks could be punished for staying out beyond curfews, for speaking critically of the government, and for being absent from work. They were not allowed to vote, testify in court, sit on juries, or carry weapons. The Fourteenth Amendment was supposed to eliminate the codes and other laws that discriminated against former slaves.

The amendment reversed the Dred Scott decision and gave blacks both state and national citizenship. In the 1833 case *Barron v. Baltimore*, the Supreme Court had ruled that the Bill of Rights did not apply to the states. Some of those who drafted the Fourteenth Amendment tried to overturn that decision—they wanted to protect blacks from state laws that denied them their rights. Their hopes were dashed by the Supreme Court's decision in the 1873 *Slaughterhouse Cases*. The Court ruled that while states could not violate the rights of national citizenship, they could regulate the rights that were part of state citizenship. According to the court, there were very few rights of national citizenship. Only in the 1920s did the Court begin to selectively apply the limitations of the Bill of Rights to the states through the "due process" clause of the Fourteenth Amendment. It wasn't until the mid-1950s, however, that the Court used the amendment to protect blacks and other groups from discrimination.

Section 2 of the Fourteenth Amendment cancels the method of counting slave populations as three-fifths of the white population within a state for purposes of voting and taxation, found in Article 1, Section 2 of the Constitution. If a state proceeds to deny adult male citizens the right to vote in state or federal elections, the state's representation in the House may be reduced. The amount of the reduction is calculated by comparing the number of those denied the vote to the total number of adult male citizens in the state.

If freed slaves were unable to vote in the South but were fully counted as members of Southern states, the number of Southern whites in the House of Representatives would increase. To prevent the South from regaining political power in Congress, the Republicans had to ensure that blacks could vote. They knew the freed slaves would not support Democratic candidates whose party had kept them in bondage for so long. In 1862, the 242 seats in the House of Representatives were redistributed by law to adjust for population changes within the thirty-eight states. In practical terms, by counting blacks as citizens, the former Confederate states were entitled to fifty-eight seats. If they did not let blacks vote, they would have only thirty-eight seats. This section of the article, however, was never carried out. Until its withdrawal in 1877, the U.S. Army of occupation in the South—not the Fourteenth Amendment—secured the rights of blacks. By then, the Democrats had regained strength in Congress, and politicians focused on other issues.

Section 3 states that any member of the Confederacy who took an oath to support the Constitution and then rebelled against the Union is barred from serving in state or federal office. By a two-thirds vote in each House, Congress can remove this political disability.

Probably no more than 1,500 people were affected by Section 3. It was included to prevent the return to power of Southern politicians who would not respect black civil rights. By 1872, this disqualification was ended.

According to Section 4, the Government of the United States pledges to pay back the money it borrowed to finance the Civil War, as well as to pay pensions and bonuses owed to those who helped the Union win the war. The Government will not honor the war debts of the Confederacy nor will claims be paid for the loss of slaves; such debts are no longer valid.

Section 4 prevented Southern financial losses from becoming political issues in the future. It was the least controversial part of the amendment.

With thirty-seven states in the Union, twenty-eight were needed for ratification. Only in 1868, when Congress made acceptance of the Fourteenth Amendment a condition for readmission to the Union, did enough Southern states approve the amendment for it to be added to the Constitution. First proposed in June 1866, the amendment was finally ratified in July 1868.

In 1868, Republican Ulysses S. Grant was elected president by only about 300,000 votes—a sign that the Democratic party was gaining strength. For the Republicans to remain in power, they needed the Northern black vote. Only in the New England states (except Connecticut) were blacks permitted to vote. In 1867, voters in a number of Northern states had turned down measures to follow New England's example.

Under these circumstances, it was politically desirable for the Republicans in Congress to act quickly to propose a black voting rights amendment before the Democratic party returned to its full strength in the House and Senate with the readmission of the Southern states. Some members of Congress also supported the amendment as a matter of conscience.

Senators and representatives debated whether to include the right to hold office in the amendment they were drafting.

In 1868, Georgia had expelled more than twenty-four black lawmakers, and Congress responded by placing the state under military rule. Other members of Congress would have included a section to outlaw state tests for property ownership, the ability to read, and proof of citizenship. Some wanted to give the vote to women as well. The leadership chose a narrower, more attainable goal. They wanted most of all to secure the black male voters.

The amendment was ratified on February 3, 1870, after four remaining Southern states (Georgia, Mississippi, Texas, and Virginia) were compelled to accept it as the price of readmission to the Union. This was the first of several steps the federal government would eventually take to broaden the nation's voting population at the expense of the states. Until then, the states had set the qualifications for voting and regulated where and when elections were held.

Once federal troops were withdrawn from the South in the late 1870s, Southern governments came under the control of white Southern Democrats. They passed a series of Jim Crow laws, which discriminated against blacks. Attendance at public schools and the use of public facilities such as railroads, restaurants, and hotels were segregated by race. In 1896, the Supreme Court's decision in *Plessy v. Ferguson* upheld these laws. A number of legal maneuvers, such as tests for literacy (the ability to read) and acts of physical violence were used to keep blacks from voting.

Such matters stayed the same until the 1930s, when blacks began to sue in federal court to reclaim their rights. One result was the Supreme Court's 1954 landmark decision in *Brown v. Board of Education* to let blacks attend the same schools as whites. In the 1960s, the civil rights movement gained momentum, spurring passage of a number of civil rights and voting acts to correct past injustices and two more amendments to the Constitution.

The **TWENTY-THIRD AMENDMENT** gives citizens in the District of Columbia the right to vote in presidential elections and allows them representation for that purpose equal to that of the least populated state in the Union. Congress is given the power to pass laws to carry out the amendment.

James Madison recommended that residents of the District should "have their voice in the election of the Government which is to exercise authority over them." Voting rights, however, had always been exercised within states. The District, established in 1790, was not a state, so its inhabitants could not elect members of the government. As long as most people living in the District eventually returned to their home states, the problem could be ignored. However, with the enormous growth of the government in the 1930s and 1940s, the District gained a large permanent population.

By the early 1960s, temporary residents—about one-fifth of the District's 553,000 people—voted by absentee ballots issued in their home states. Absentee ballots are pieces of paper that list candidates for public office and are mailed to voters who will be out of their home state on Election Day. The permanent residents of the District—most of whom were black—could not use absentee ballots. The Twenty-third Amendment finally gave them the right to vote for president and vice president. It was ratified on March 29, 1961, about nine months after being submitted to the states.

The **TWENTY-FOURTH AMENDMENT** forbids the federal government or the states from making citizens pay poll taxes or other taxes in order to vote in national elections. Congress has the power to enforce this amendment by law if necessary.

Poll taxes were once used to prove that colonial and revolutionary voters were financially independent and responsible citizens. After the Civil War, Southern officials used them to keep blacks and poor whites from voting. Senator Spessard Holland, a Florida Democrat, had been trying for eleven years to persuade Congress to approve an anti–poll tax amendment. In 1960, he was able to attach his proposal to another that dealt with temporary vacancies in the House and giving the vote in federal elections to residents of the District of Columbia. Holland's measure was sacrificed to secure passage of the Twenty-third Amendment. In 1962, when it was reintroduced, only five states still had a poll tax, and the amount charged was usually one or two dollars, payable months in advance. However, the U.S. Commission on Civil Rights found that the tax did discourage voter turnout by discriminating against blacks and poor whites. Despite Southern Democrats' votes against the amendment, Congress was able to propose the measure to the states in August 1962. It was ratified January 23, 1964.

VOTES FOR WOMEN

Women were another disadvantaged group denied the protection of the Bill of Rights and prevented from voting. Women were treated as dependents. According to John Adams, women and children lacked independent judgment, and "their delicacy renders them unfit for practice and experience in the great businesses of life." Women could not sue or be sued in court, sign legal documents, or own property. They were under the protection and direction of their fathers, brothers, or husbands. Nevertheless, in the period preceding the Civil War, women were active members of many social reform movements. In 1848, their campaign to receive legal rights produced New York's Married Women's Property Act, giving them some control over their own holdings. By 1900, every state had similar laws.

Gaining the right to vote involved a longer, more difficult

struggle. Just three months after the 1848 New York law was passed, the first Women's Rights Convention was held at Seneca Falls, New York. Led by Lucretia Mott and Elizabeth Cady Stanton, it issued a Declaration of Sentiments, drawn from the Declaration of Independence, claiming full citizenship for women, including the right to vote. Over the next twenty years, women's organizations campaigned for voting rights. Especially disappointing was their failure to convince Congress to include women in the Fourteenth and Fifteenth Amendments. Women's rights leader Susan B. Anthony angrily vowed "to cut off this right arm of mine before I will demand the ballot for the Negro and not the woman." Women had spearheaded the abolitionist movement. They were hurt to be told that giving them political rights would endanger passage of the two amendments they worked so hard to achieve.

Another major setback occurred in 1875, when the Supreme Court decided the case of *Minor v. Happersett*. The justices rejected Virginia Minor's argument that denying women

☆ ══════ ☆

A cartoon of 1859 represented the first Woman's Rights Convention in 1848 in Seneca Falls, New York. The men in the galleries jeered and hooted at the women speakers.

the right to vote deprived them of their rights of citizenship under the Fourteenth Amendment. A constitutional amendment would be needed to overrule the Court's decision. In 1890, the National American Woman Suffrage Association was formed to make sure the new amendment passed. Meanwhile some gains were made: as early as 1869, the Wyoming Territory had allowed women to vote. By 1897, twenty-seven states had passed similar laws. When Congress finally drafted a women's suffrage amendment in 1919, seventeen states already allowed women to vote in all elections. Another thirteen states let them participate only in national elections, while eighteen states still denied them voting rights.

The **NINETEENTH AMENDMENT** grants women the right to vote and gives Congress the power to pass whatever laws may be needed to secure this right.

For thirty-three years, members of Congress had been proposing amendments to give women the vote, but none was passed until 1919. Despite support from President Woodrow Wilson and former president Theodore Roosevelt, the Senate could not muster the needed two-thirds majority. Some senators opposed the amendment because they felt that the national government should not interfere with states' rights to regulate elections. Southern Democrats did not want black women to vote. Northern conservatives feared that women voters would support better working conditions for female factory workers. In 1919, a year after the end of World War I, the Susan B. Anthony amendment, as it was called at the time, was finally sent to the states for ratification. Women had distinguished themselves in the war effort, and it was no longer possible to ignore their demand to vote. On August 26, 1920, Secretary of State Bainbridge Colby certified the Nineteenth Amendment.

LOWERING THE VOTING AGE

For about 180 years, Americans defined adults as people at least twenty-one years old. This meant that under existing laws, eighteen-, nineteen-, and twenty-year-olds were not permitted to vote. Nevertheless, as time passed, they could legally get drivers' licenses, marry, and serve in the nation's armed forces. Beginning in 1942, during World War II, amendments to lower the voting age were repeatedly introduced—and defeated—in Congress. Presidents Dwight D. Eisenhower, Lyndon B. Johnson, and Richard M. Nixon continued to pressure Congress to act, reasoning that if young men were old enough to risk their lives for their country, they were old enough to vote.

The **TWENTY-SIXTH AMENDMENT** permits citizens who are eighteen years of age or older to vote in national and state elections. Congress has the power to pass laws to enforce this requirement.

In the 1960s, many young people protested American involvement in the Vietnam War. The protesters argued that they had not even been able to choose the members of the government who were sending them to fight in Southeast Asia. Meanwhile the baby boom generation was coming of age, which vastly increased the number of potential voters. Congress reacted to the protesters and the boomers by passing the Voting Rights Act in 1970, which lowered the voting age. Then the Supreme Court ruled in *Oregon v. Mitchell* that young people could vote in federal elections, but that an act of Congress could not make changes in state and local election laws. As a result of the Court's decision, states would have to keep separate sets of records for federal and state elections, a great inconvenience. Alternatively, the states could change their election laws. (Nine states already let eighteen-, nineteen-, or twenty-year-olds vote

☆ ━━━━━━ ☆

Confusion and protests on the voting laws between the states and the federal government finally led to the Twenty-sixth Amendment.

in elections. The age limit, however, was not uniform) A constitutional amendment seemed to be the best solution. Three months after the Supreme Court's decision, Congress sent the Twenty-sixth Amendment to the states. It was ratified on June 30, 1971, making it the fastest ratification of a constitutional amendment in American history.

☆   ☆   ☆

Not only have amendments been used to extend the benefits of citizenship to previously neglected groups of Americans, they have also corrected structural problems that arose after the Constitution was put into effect. It was this type of amendment, and not changes to broaden personal and voting rights, that the framers had in mind when they wrote Article 5 of the Constitution. Thus, when the presidency developed flaws, the amending process was activated.

FOUR

ALTERING THE PRESIDENCY

After the Constitution was written, changes were made to correct defects, record customs that developed over time, clarify principles, and fill in omissions. Early in the nation's history, it was obvious that the procedure to elect the president and vice president was flawed and had to be fixed. Later, it seemed desirable to make a long-standing tradition binding and limit the president's term of service. Because the Constitution was unclear, another custom developed that was later recognized in an amendment: when a president died in office, the vice president became president, not just a caretaker or acting president. Finally, arrangements had to made in the event of disabling presidential illnesses and vacancies in the vice presidency—problems not covered in the Constitution.

ELECTING THE PRESIDENT AND VICE PRESIDENT

As a result of a series of compromises, the framers created a novel method of electing the president. The president was to be chosen by electors in each state, with the number of a state's electors being equal to the number of senators and representatives it sent to Congress. At first, about half the electors were chosen by state legislatures; the others, by the people. (Before long, citizens in most states, rather than legislators, voted for electors, thereby introducing the popular election of the president.) The framers feared that a president seeking reelection might try to influence electors to vote for him by offering them government jobs. To prevent this, the Constitution barred electors from serving in the federal government.

The Constitution required that each elector cast two votes for president. Because the framers feared that there would be too many candidates, one vote had to be given to someone living outside the elector's home state. Otherwise, electors would favor their own states' candidates, making it difficult for anyone to win the election. On the other hand, the framers would not permit the electors to deliberately combine their votes to ensure a particular candidate's victory, the way political parties do. (Political parties are organizations that sponsor candidates for public office and help them get elected.) The framers opposed political parties because they did not want any political group in the nation to become too powerful. Thus, the electors were required to vote in their home states, rather than at some central meeting place.

The candidate with a majority of the votes would become president, and the runner-up, vice president. In the event of a tie or a failure to get a majority of electoral votes, the House of Representatives would choose a president from the five leading candidates. Having five competitors gave the small states a stake in the election and prevented the four largest states from dominating the proceedings. Each state would have one vote. Again, the runner-up would become vice president.

This method of electing the president did not work once George Washington retired as the nation's first president. During his term in office, political parties had developed. If each elector cast two votes without indicating which was for president and which was for vice president, a number of complications could arise. For example, in the election of 1796, the system produced a president of one party, Federalist John Adams, and a vice president of another party, Democratic-Republican Thomas Jefferson.

In the election of 1800, Democratic-Republican electors cast one of their two ballots for presidential candidate Thomas

Jefferson and the other for vice presidential candidate Aaron Burr. Although they defeated their Federalist opponents John Adams and Charles C. Pinckney, Jefferson and Burr each received seventy-three votes. The Federalists avoided a tie between their candidates by having one elector fail to cast his vote for Pinckney. The Democratic-Republicans bungled similar arrangements. Some electors thought others were discarding a vice presidential vote, but no one did it.

Since Jefferson and Burr had tied, the House of Representatives would decide the election. At this point, Burr could have declined to run against Jefferson, but he did not. Since Federalists in Congress consistently divided their vote between the two men, Congress balloted thirty-six times before Jefferson gained a majority of the votes and became president. Burr, as runner-up, became vice president. The election of 1800 triggered passage of the Twelfth Amendment.

According to the **TWELFTH AMENDMENT**, electors cast separate ballots for president and vice president, which are counted separately in front of the members of Congress by the president of the Senate. A majority of the vote is needed to win.

As a result of the amendment, ties between presidential and vice presidential candidates could never again happen.

The Twelfth Amendment provides that if no presidential candidate receives a majority of the votes cast by electors, the House of Representatives, with two-thirds of its membership present, shall choose the winner from the top three candidates by majority vote. Each state has one vote. If the House cannot choose a president before the swearing-in date, the vice president will temporarily act as president.

The number of candidates was reduced from five to three because the mechanism for selecting a vice president had also changed. The small states were unhappy about their loss of influence, but the change was made despite their objections.

> *The vice presidential candidate with a majority of the electors' votes wins. In the event of a tie, the Senate, with two-thirds of its membership present, will make the choice between the two leading candidates.*

When the Twelfth Amendment was first proposed in 1802, its opponents complained that it would weaken the vice presidency. The office would attract less-qualified candidates and become the object of political bargains among different sections of the country. This is, in fact, what happened. Many second-rate politicians became vice president in deals to balance the ticket between North and South or East and West, to widen the party's appeal to the voters. In 1802, the Twelfth Amendment failed by one vote in the Senate. It passed in 1803 and was ratified by thirteen of the seventeen states in 1804, in time for the upcoming presidential election.

TERM LIMITS FOR THE PRESIDENT

George Washington began the custom for American presidents to serve no more than two terms in office. After much debate, the framers set four-year terms for presidents, with no limit on the number of times a president could be returned to office. In 1788, Washington explained in a letter that it would be unwise to deny the country "the service of any one man who on some great emergency shall be deemed universally most capable of serving the public." Since the Constitution went into effect, more than two hundred proposals changing the president's term in office had been submitted to Congress, but they were ignored. If a candidate was reelected to office, he simply followed George Washington's example and retired at the end of his second term.

Emergencies arose in the 1930s and 1940s that led Democratic president Franklin D. Roosevelt to break with tradition and be elected to office four times in a row. In the 1930s, a severe economic downturn, known as the Great Depression, brought business to a halt. Millions were jobless. Private charities and local agencies were overwhelmed with requests from distressed Americans for help. During his first two terms in office, Roosevelt set up national programs to offer relief, help the nation recover, and reform the way the nation did business. At the end of the decade, World War II erupted in Europe, and the president expected that the United States would be drawn into the conflict sooner or later. Thus, he chose to run for a third term. By 1944, American troops were fighting all over the

☆ ══════ ☆

In January 1945 President Roosevelt pledged a just and durable peace to end World War II. His health failing, he died on April 12 of that year.

globe. Roosevelt agreed to run again to bring the war to an end, but three months after he was elected to his fourth term, he died. Vice President Harry S. Truman took over Roosevelt's duties as president. Congress sought to prevent future presidents from following Roosevelt's four-term example.

The **TWENTY-SECOND AMENDMENT** restores tradition by restricting presidents to two terms in office. Vice presidents who complete more than two years of a deceased president's term can only hold office for one more term. The states have seven years to approve this change. It does not apply to Harry Truman or any other president in office before the amendment is ratified.

In 1947, Republicans held a majority of seats in the legislature for the first time since 1928. They were determined to pass a presidential term-limit amendment to prevent future presidents from following Roosevelt's example. Republican Louis Graham of Pennsylvania justified the amendment, stating, "We have seen the evil of perpetuation of centralization of government, of control through great bureaucracies, appointments of courts and control of our foreign relations, all due to the build-up, accumulated potency [power] of one man remaining too long in public office." Democrat Sam Rayburn of Texas thought Congress should wait and take up the question when the Roosevelt experience was not on everyone's mind. He opposed the amendment, arguing, "For the people to have the privilege of choosing whom they please to be their leader is democracy, real democracy, in action." (The Democrats also pointed out that members of Congress had yet to limit their own terms.) Before the year was over, Congress proposed the amendment to the states. By 1951, thirty-six of the forty-eight existing states had given their approval, and the Twenty-second Amendment was added to the Constitution.

REPLACING PRESIDENTS AND VICE PRESIDENTS DUE TO DEATH, RESIGNATION, OR ILLNESS

The **TWENTY-FIFTH AMENDMENT** outlines the procedures to be followed if the office of president or vice president is vacant or if the president is disabled.

The Constitution was vague about the procedures to be followed when a president died, resigned, or became too ill to carry out his duties while in office. It also made no provision for replacing a vice president who took over when a president died. For the framers, who were eager to go home, the vice presidency was simply a last-minute solution to the problems of electing the president and providing a presiding officer for the Senate. They did not anticipate that their solution would create a new set of difficulties.

The first section of the Twenty-fifth Amendment clarifies that the vice president becomes president upon the death or resignation of the president.

In 1841, when President William Henry Harrison died a month after taking office, it was unclear whether his vice president, John Tyler, became president for the remainder of Harrison's term or served merely as a caretaker until a new president could be chosen. According to historians, the framers meant for the vice president to serve as a temporary replacement until new elections could be held. Tyler, however, insisted upon being sworn in as president. Future vice presidents in similar situations followed his example. The Twenty-fifth Amendment belatedly approved their actions.

> *The second section of the Twenty-fifth Amendment provides that when the office of vice president is vacant, the president nominates a replacement who must be approved by a majority vote in both the House and Senate.*

There were sixteen vice presidential vacancies between 1812 and 1961. No one had given the matter much thought until 1963, when Lyndon B. Johnson became president after the assassination of John F. Kennedy. Johnson himself had already suffered a heart attack and his potential presidential successors—the presiding officers of the House and Senate—were elderly men. In view of the continuing tension between the Soviet Union and the United States, the nation could ill afford to risk having them as replacements for the president in the event of an international crisis. Thus, the Twenty-fifth Amendment was introduced in Congress shortly after President Johnson took the oath of office. Because of disagreements among members of Congress, however, it was not proposed to the states until 1965. It was ratified two years later.

The vice presidential vacancy provision produced an unintended result: the nation's first unelected president and vice president. During the fall of 1973, Richard Nixon's vice president, Spiro T. Agnew—accused of receiving bribes while governor of Maryland—resigned from office. President Nixon nominated Republican representative Gerald R. Ford of Michigan as Agnew's replacement, and Ford was approved by Congress. Then in the summer of 1974, President Nixon himself resigned rather than face proceedings to remove him from office. (He had tried to prevent the government from prosecuting members of his staff who were linked to a break-in at Democratic National Headquarters at the Watergate building complex.) Upon becoming president, Ford chose Republican governor of New York Nelson A. Rockefeller to serve as his vice president.

The third section of the Twenty-fifth Amendment states that the vice president shall serve as acting president whenever the president sends the presiding officers of the House and Senate a letter stating that he is unable to carry out the duties of his office. The president will again take up his responsibilities upon notifying these congressional leaders by letter of his recovery.

The fourth section of the Twenty-fifth Amendment allows the vice president to serve as acting president when the vice president and a majority of the heads of government departments, or any other group that Congress chooses by law, send the presiding officers of the Congress a letter stating that the president is disabled. When the president is recovered, he transmits a letter notifying the congressional leaders of such. If the vice president and heads of departments, or another group chosen by Congress, disagree, they have four days in which to notify the presiding officers that they believe the president is still disabled. Then Congress shall decide the issue, assembling within forty-eight hours if the legislature is not in session. The lawmakers have twenty-one days to determine whether the vice president should continue as acting president or whether the president can carry out his duties. A two-thirds vote in both houses is required.

The Twenty-fifth Amendment finally solved the problem of presidential disability where previous efforts had failed. In the 1880s, for example, Congress—prompted by President James A. Garfield's hopeless two-month struggle to survive an assassin's bullet—considered a constitutional amendment outlining the steps to be followed when a president was seriously ill. No action was taken. As a result, in 1919, when President Woodrow Wilson suffered a crippling stroke, the government nearly stopped functioning. The president remained isolated from the public for months, scrawling his signature on papers handed to him by his wife, Edith. She decided what issues should be brought to his attention. Vice President Thomas R. Marshall did not want to appear to be usurping Wilson's office, so he refused to take over. Wilson later criticized his cabinet, because

☆ ═══════ ☆

After President Wilson's crippling stroke in the fall of 1919,
his wife, Edith, became both his nurse and his executive secretary.

the heads of departments had tried to keep things going on
their own.

The problem of presidential disability was ignored again
until the mid-1950s when President Dwight D. Eisenhower developed several serious illnesses. Unable to convince Congress
to amend the Constitution, he exchanged letters with his vice
president, Richard M. Nixon, in which they established the
procedures to be followed if he became disabled again. These
were made public on March 3, 1958. Other presidents followed
his example until the Twenty-fifth Amendment eliminated the
need for such arrangements.

☆   ☆   ☆

The remaining amendments to the Constitution concerned the
federal courts and Congress, making them more responsive to
the wishes of the states and the people. They also modernized
the federal government.

FIVE

ADJUSTING THE COURTS AND CONGRESS

Only one amendment, passed early in the nation's history, affected the federal courts. Six others, all ratified in the twentieth century, altered Congress. While the court amendment took power away from the national government, the congressional amendments, for the most part, had the opposite effect: the legislature was given more to do, was made more accountable to the public, and was updated.

LIMITING THE TYPES OF CASES TRIED IN FEDERAL COURTS

According to the **ELEVENTH AMENDMENT**, federal courts can no longer decide lawsuits against states brought by citizens of other states or citizens of other nations.

The Eleventh Amendment was passed to overturn a Supreme Court decision involving Robert Farquhar, a South Carolina merchant who sold supplies to the government of Georgia during the War of Independence. Farquhar died in 1784, before he was paid. In his will, he appointed his friend Alexander Chisholm to settle his affairs. Chisholm brought a lawsuit to recover debts the state of Georgia owed to Farquhar. Article 3 of the Constitution let citizens of one state sue another state in federal court, thereby enabling Chisholm to bring his case before the Supreme Court. In 1793, the Court ruled in his favor, and the decision in *Chisholm v. Georgia* created an uproar. (The Georgia legislature even discussed the possibility of hanging any official who tried to enforce the ruling!) State governments feared they would be sued by British and Loyalist creditors to recover lands seized and given to new owners during the Revolutionary War. Southern states, in particular, resented the decision. They had grown suspicious of the federal government and feared it would gradually destroy their remaining powers under the Constitution.

In 1794, Congress proposed the Eleventh Amendment as a remedy. It was ratified on February 7, 1795, but not certified until January 8, 1798. The states had delayed informing the federal government of their approval, and the administration of John Adams stalled certification until Congress questioned him on the amendment's status. Adams wanted to carve out a role for the presidency in the amending process. His successors did not follow his example.

PROGRESSIVE REFORMS: AN OVERVIEW

The Progressive Era (from about 1890 to 1918) produced several important amendments affecting Congress, as well as the Nineteenth Amendment, which gave women the vote. Passing laws as well as amendments, Progressives actively used the power of government to improve conditions. They targeted big corporations that were amassing wealth by exploiting immigrant laborers forced to work in unsanitary conditions, corrupt politicians who bought and sold votes, and injurious private conduct such as drinking alcoholic beverages. As a result of the Progressive crusade, Congress passed laws to regulate railroad rates, to protect consumers from impure foods and drugs, and to make industries more competitive. Congress also offered a number of amendments to make government more responsive to the needs of the people and, for the first time, to regulate people's private behavior.

GIVING CONGRESS THE POWER TO IMPOSE INCOME TAXES

The framers of the Constitution apportioned taxes among the states according to the size of the states' populations. Traditionally, the federal government raised the money it needed by placing fees on foreign goods brought in for sale in the United States and by taxing a few specific locally made items. The taxes fell more heavily on the poor than on the rich, who could more easily afford them. Corporations benefited, as high fees on foreign goods encouraged American manufacturing.

The nation's first income tax law, passed in 1861, helped the government offset the costs of the Civil War. The law expired in 1872. As a result of an economic slump in 1893, the government once again did not have enough money to meet its expenses. So in 1894, Congress wrote a new income tax law that required people who earned more than $4,000 a year to pay 2 percent of their earnings to the federal government; corporations were also taxed at the 2 percent rate. Progressives thought an income tax would be fairer to most Americans than other forms of taxation. Gradually, it would let the government lower fees imposed on foreign goods, and it would equalize somewhat the distribution of wealth within the nation. Their views were not shared by everyone. In the 1895 case, *Pollock v. Farmers' Loan and Trust Co.*, the Supreme Court ruled that income taxes violated the Constitution because they were based on earnings, not population. Charles Pollock was a bank shareholder who sued to stop his bank from paying the tax.

The **Sixteenth Amendment** gives Congress the power to impose income taxes based on individual and corporate earnings rather than on the population of the states.

Like the Eleventh Amendment, the Sixteenth Amendment was introduced in Congress to overturn a Supreme Court decision. Between 1895 and 1909, corporations and other special-interest groups who benefited from high fees on foreign goods thwarted the Progressives' attempts to win congressional approval for the new amendment. (By 1909, 1 percent of the nation's businesses manufactured 44 percent of its products.) Public opinion, however, rallied behind the Progressives' cause. Finally, in 1909, Congress offered the Sixteenth Amendment— supported by Presidents Theodore Roosevelt and William H. Taft—to the states. On February 25, 1913, Secretary of State Philander C. Knox certified that it had been accepted by the thirty-six states needed for ratification. In effect, the amendment broadened Congress's lawmaking powers to include levying income taxes.

DIRECT ELECTION OF UNITED STATES SENATORS

Political corruption was another target of the Progressive movement. State lawmakers and their political parties catered to business and other special-interest groups at the expense of the public. The politicians received large donations from corporations and businessmen for passing favorable laws and securing government contracts for them. The corrupting influence of corporate political power had to be curbed. One way to accomplish this was to let the people elect the members of the Senate.

The framers of the Constitution had given the states equal representation in the Senate and let each state legislature choose two senators. This was a compromise to compensate the small states for the decision to make the number of representatives in Congress dependent on each state's population and to allow them to be elected by the people. The framers never anticipated that state legislatures would select senators who served private business interests rather than the public interest. Nevertheless, following the Civil War, when fortunes were made as the nation became industrialized, the parties' wealthiest contributors frequently were made senators. It was no wonder that the Senate was known as the Millionaires' Club. Professional politicians like Thomas C. Platt of New York were chosen as well. Platt became a senator because he controlled the state legislature, with backing from business and support from immigrant voters. Progressive reformers challenged these powerful and influential men by proposing the direct election of senators by the people of each state.

The **SEVENTEENTH AMENDMENT** provides that each state's two senators are elected directly by the people, defined as those qualified to vote for the most numerous house in the state legislature. The senators still serve six-year terms and cast one vote apiece on matters before the Senate. When vacancies occur, the state governor holds a special election for a replacement unless directed by the state legislature to make a temporary appointment until an election can be held at a later date. The terms and election of senators chosen before the amendment was ratified remain unchanged.

As early as 1826, Congress received a proposal for the popular election of senators. Similar proposals were made in the 1850s and 1860s, but nothing had been done. In the 1890s, with the publication of a series of newspaper articles exposing corporations' influence over the Senate, support for a direct-election amendment became more widespread. Between 1893 and 1905, thirty-one of the forty-five states actively sought such an amendment. Some even suggested that a convention be called to propose the change. The Senate, however, blocked every proposal for constitutional reform.

Meanwhile, at the turn of the century, Oregon found a way to give voters a say in the selection of their senators, and the idea soon spread to other states. These states held primaries in which voters could nominate or express their preference for a political party's candidate for the Senate. The state legislature was then required to elect the winner of the primary. By 1911, more than half the states were using this system. Still, it did not provide uniformity, since not all the states adopted it or used the same primary system. Also, it did not prevent some conservative senators from being chosen by state lawmakers who were opposed to Progressive reforms. The 1910 elections, however, produced ten senators elected by the people. These senators' votes helped to secure passage of the Seventeenth Amendment. On May 13, 1912, it was proposed by Congress to the states and was ratified April 8, 1913.

THE BAN AGAINST ALCOHOLIC BEVERAGES

Progressives wanted to eliminate personal as well as political corruption. They argued that drunkenness was harmful to society, that it prevented people from working and broke up families. Like most Americans at that time, they believed that alcoholism was a moral flaw, a character weakness. (Today, it is seen as an illness.) However, Progressives did not invent Prohibition (the ban on the manufacture and sale of alcoholic beverages). In 1851, Portland businessman Neal Dow helped push through the first state Prohibition statute, known as the Maine Law. He went on to found the Prohibition Party in 1869. Still in existence today, it is the nation's oldest minor, or third, political party. Other groups, such as the Woman's Christian Temperance Union (WTCU) and the Anti-Saloon League of America (ASL), founded in the 1890s, also crusaded against drinking and drunkenness. Carrie Nation of the ASL made headlines when she burst into saloons or barrooms with her hatchet to destroy their wares. Emma Willard of the WCTU also encouraged her followers to protest in saloons.

Collectively, members of the Prohibition movement—mostly white, middle-class, rural Protestants—were known as

☆ ══════ ☆

Carrie Nation's temperance crusade is illustrated in a 1901 cartoon.

"drys." Progressives joined with them to spearhead the drive for an amendment to the Constitution to ban drinking. The drys developed educational programs for schools about the evils of drinking, and they worked to elect state and local officials who shared their views. They targeted large cities as the object of their crusade. In the cities could be found about 14.5 million new immigrants who had arrived in the United States between 1900 and 1915. Most were crammed into unhealthy slums, and often, drinking in saloons offered them an escape from their misery and a chance to socialize with friends. City politicians, needing the immigrant vote, were not about to shut down these taverns. They and their supporters became known as the "wets."

The **EIGHTEENTH AMENDMENT** seeks to end drunkenness by banning drinks that contain alcohol.

The first Prohibition amendment had been proposed in 1876 and was reintroduced eighteen more times by 1913. Between 1913 and 1917, thirty-nine more proposals had been presented to Congress. By that time, twenty-one states had already adopted Prohibition. Nevertheless, an amendment was needed to promote uniformity throughout the nation; otherwise, people could travel out of state to buy liquor. America's entry into World War I in 1917 helped the Prohibitionists. Grain and sugar used to make alcoholic beverages had to be diverted to feed American troops. Also, beer became less popular because it was the national drink of enemy Germany. In the congressional elections of 1916, the drys finally outnumbered the wets two to one, providing enough votes for the Prohibition amendment to be offered to the states.

Section 2 of the Eighteenth Amendment lets Congress and the states share the power to enforce the amendment.

This sharing of power was a novel feature in the amendment, but it prevented states from complaining that Congress was interfering with their police powers—their responsibility for the health, safety, and welfare of their citizens. On October 28, 1919, Congress passed the Volstead Act (National Prohibition Enforcement Act). This law set the standards for determining which beverages would be considered alcoholic, named a federal agency to enforce the amendment, and established fines and prison terms for those who violated the amendment. Like other Progressive amendments, the Eighteenth Amendment broadened Congress's lawmaking power.

> *Section 3 of the Eighteenth Amendment requires state legislatures to ratify the amendment within seven years of the date on which Congress offers it to the states.*

This was the first amendment to include a time limit. It was added by the wets, in hopes of preventing ratification, but they were soon disappointed. The amendment was officially proposed on December 18, 1917, and ratified by the needed thirty-six states on January 16, 1919.

LIFTING THE BAN ON ALCOHOLIC BEVERAGES

The Eighteenth Amendment was unique: it was the only addition to the Constitution that regulated private conduct. It was also the only amendment to be repealed, or canceled, by another amendment, the Twenty-first.

Prohibition had failed. Many moderate drinkers who supported the amendment did not really want to give up drinking altogether. In private, many Americans defied the Eighteenth Amendment. Since they could no longer go to a liquor store, bar, or tavern, they made their own "bathtub gin" or turned to illegal suppliers. "Bootleggers" secretly sold them bottles of liquor or wine; "rumrunners" sneaked in cases of forbidden beverages from abroad. Also, determined drinkers could go to "speakeasies," private clubs that sold illegal drinks. Federal agents could not possibly arrest all the people who broke the law; they did, however, go after the gangsters who had gained control of the illegal liquor trade. One of the most notorious was Al Capone, who waged a series of violent gang wars to drive his rivals out of town so he could run Chicago's bootleg-

Bootleggers managed to supply liquor to Americans from rumrunners who delivered the liquor just miles off our shores.

ging operations. By 1929, thirty repeal amendments had been offered in Congress.

Section 1 of the **TWENTY-FIRST AMENDMENT** repeals the Eighteenth Amendment.

Two major changes in the United States contributed to the repeal of the Eighteenth Amendment in 1933. One was the Great Depression. It had forced many businesses to close and put millions of people out of work. The sale and manufacture of alcoholic beverages was welcomed because it would create jobs and give people money to spend. Among those who would benefit were farmers who grew the grain, brewers and distillers who made beer and liquor, and railroaders and truckers who shipped the products to market.

The other change took place in Congress. By the 1920s, for the first time in the nation's history, a majority of Americans were no longer living in rural areas. They had moved to cities, where support for Prohibition was weakest. Seats in the House were redistributed to reflect this population shift. As a result, many of the lawmakers were more willing to vote for repeal. The presidential election of 1932 was seen as a contest between the Republican drys and the Democrat wets. The Democrats won overwhelmingly. The Republicans, however, realized long before Election Day that Prohibition was no longer a popular cause.

Section 2 of the Twenty-first Amendment makes it illegal to sell or ship alcoholic beverages in states, possessions, or territories of the United States in violation of their laws.

Section 2 helped enforce state prohibition laws. When repeal went into effect, Kansas, Oklahoma, and Mississippi chose to remain dry states.

Section 3 requires states to hold conventions in order to ratify the Twenty-first Amendment. They have seven years from the time Congress submits this proposal to the states.

The Twenty-first Amendment was the first and only time a state-convention procedure was used to obtain the states' approval. To end Prohibition, both wets and drys preferred letting specially elected state conventions, rather than state legislatures, make the decision. Believing that most Americans supported the repeal, the wets wanted to bypass state legislatures, as many were still dominated by rural, dry politicians. The wets thought popularly elected conventions would be more likely to accept the amendment. The drys in state legislatures supported the conventions because they could avoid having to take a public stand on the controversial issue of repeal. The amendment was ratified by the necessary thirty-six states on December 5, 1933.

ADJUSTING FEDERAL TERMS OF OFFICE AND ARRANGING ALTERNATE METHODS OF CHOOSING A PRESIDENT

For many years, Progressives had wanted to correct some technical flaws in the Constitution. With Democrats controlling Congress in 1930, the Twentieth Amendment was finally prepared for presentation to the states. At the time, it was known as the Norris amendment because Progressive senator George W. Norris, a Republican from Nebraska, had worked so hard to get it drafted and accepted. Later, it came to be called the Lame-Duck Amendment for reasons soon to be made clear.

The TWENTIETH AMENDMENT is remembered for changing the dates on which government officials leave office, although it also clarifies some procedures for replacing a president.

Section 1 of the Twentieth Amendment states that presidential and vice presidential terms in office will end at noon on January 20, with congressional terms being completed on January 3 in the years when such terms normally end. Their successors' terms will begin on the same days.

The framers provided that the Constitution would go into effect when ratified by nine states; this took place in June 1788. The Confederation Congress managed national affairs in the meantime. Because travel was difficult and time-consuming, and elections first had to be held, this Congress called for the new government to be sworn in on the first Wednesday in March 1789, which happened to be March 4. Afterward, the starting date could not be changed without an amendment, as the length of presidential and congressional terms were fixed by the Constitution. This arrangement produced a number of unexpected problems. For example, a newly elected president had to wait more than three months before taking office.

Section 2 of the amendment requires Congress to meet at least once a year, the session starting at noon on January 3 unless the lawmakers set another day by law.

The Constitution had fixed the first Monday in December as the date for Congress to meet. By custom, Congress had a long session and a short session. The long session began in December of an odd-numbered year and ended in July of an even-numbered year. Following congressional elections in November, the outgoing Congress met again for a short session from December to March. It was known as a "lame-duck" session since many members were simply serving out the rest of their terms before leaving office. As a result, members of Congresses elected in odd-numbered years did not meet until thirteen months after their election.

A lot of mischief could occur during lame-duck sessions. In 1801, for example, members of the defeated Federalist party in Congress increased the number of federal judges and appointed their supporters to the new posts. The victorious Democratic-Republicans in Congress had to wait thirteen months to undo the Federalists' changes. The Twentieth Amendment rescheduled Congressional sessions so that the lawmakers would meet just two months after they were elected.

According to Section 3 of the Twentieth Amendment, if the incoming president dies before being sworn in, the incoming vice president becomes president. If the president has not yet been chosen or fails to qualify, the incoming vice president shall act as president until a president has qualified. If neither an incoming president nor vice president qualifies, then Congress will choose a temporary replacement until they have qualified.

According to Section 4 of the Twentieth Amendment, when the House must choose a president or the Senate a vice president, if any of the candidates die, the lawmakers may choose their replacements.

Sections 3 and 4 were intended to solve problems arising under the Twelfth Amendment, if the House or Senate deadlocked on their choice of a president or vice president. In February 1933, a month after the Twentieth Amendment was ratified incoming president Franklin D. Roosevelt was the subject of a failed assassination attempt. Although the amendment's arrangements for presidential succession were never used, they proved to be reassuring.

The Twentieth Amendment has to be ratified within seven years after it is presented to the states.

The amendment was ratified on January 23, 1933. By May of that year, all forty-eight states had approved it.

REGULATING CONGRESSIONAL PAY INCREASES

The Twenty-seventh Amendment to the Constitution is an oddity. It was proposed as part of the Bill of Rights Congress sent to the states in 1789 but received only six state ratifications at that time. In 1873, one more state approved it, but it wasn't ratified until 1992, more than one hundred years later. As a result, this latest addition to the Constitution is actually one of the earliest amendments to be offered to the states.

The **TWENTY-SEVENTH AMENDMENT** states that a congressional election must occur before congressional pay raises may take effect.

In the 1980s and early 1990s, the public had become disgusted that members of Congress voted themselves pay increases without going on record. Congress developed a number of voting procedures that do not register individual lawmakers' positions. One such method is the teller vote, in which members of Congress walk down the aisles to be counted for or against an issue but their names are not listed. Beginning with Maine in 1983, states began to ratify the 1789 amendment. Constitutional scholars and members of Congress were divided over whether it was still valid. It did not, however, contain a seven-year time limit, as do so many modern amendments. On May 18, 1992, after accumulating the necessary thirty-eight state approvals, Chief Archivist Don W. Wilson certified the Twenty-seventh Amendment; the requirements of Article 5 had been met. Congress endorsed his decision on May 20, 1992.

☆ ☆ ☆

In the two hundred or so years that the Constitution has been in force, it has been amended only twenty-seven times. Thousands of other amendments have been rejected. To keep the Constitution up to date, Americans have developed other methods of change and adaptation.

SIX

KEEPING THE CONSTITUTION UP TO DATE

To discourage impulsive and poorly thought-out changes to the Constitution, the framers made the amending process complicated and time consuming. As a result, only twenty-seven amendments have been added to the Constitution. They have secured individuals' freedoms, extended voting rights to more citizens, and adjusted the presidency, courts, and Congress. The amendments have also served other purposes: they have corrected flaws in the framers' plan of government, clarified constitutional principles, filled in omissions, and overturned some Supreme Court decisions. As a result, a Constitution written in the eighteenth century has been adapted to the needs and conditions of the twentieth century.

SOME AMENDMENTS DEFEATED IN THE TWENTIETH CENTURY

Thousands of other amendments have been introduced in Congress since 1789. These proposals either failed to win enough votes among the lawmakers or enough ratifications by the states. The twentieth century produced its share of defeated amendments, among them measures to regulate and ban child labor, give equal rights to women, balance the federal budget, and limit the number of times members of Congress could be reelected to office.

The child labor amendment was introduced in Congress in 1924. The framers, who lived in a mostly agricultural society, could not have anticipated that children would be working in factories and mines for long hours in unsanitary conditions. This was a problem that developed in the late nineteenth and early twentieth centuries, when the United States became a highly industrialized nation. In 1920, more than one million children from ages ten to fifteen were part of the labor force. In 1918 and 1922, the Supreme Court struck down Progressive federal laws that sought to eliminate child labor. When Congress proposed an amendment to overturn the Court's decision, however, only twenty-eight states ratified it. Manufacturing interests, along with people who resented federal interference in state matters, combined to defeat the measure. By 1938, an amendment was no longer needed. During the Great Depression, unemployed adults took over many jobs previously held by children. Also, the Fair Labor Standards Act of 1938—upheld by the Supreme Court—made child labor illegal.

The first Equal Rights Amendment (ERA) was presented to Congress in 1923, but the lawmakers did not accept this proposal to treat men and women equally until 1972. Opponents objected that women would lose certain legal protections, such as limits on the amount of hours they could work and their exemption from military service. After the Civil Rights Act of 1964 banned discrimination in the workplace, the Court invalidated laws protecting women and cleared the way for the ERA to be reintroduced. The amendment prohibited federal and state governments from denying equal rights to citizens on the basis of their sex. It fell three states short of ratification. The ERA was defeated by conservatives who raised the specter of unisex bathrooms and the military draft of women. They also argued that the ERA would destroy traditional family values. Meanwhile the Supreme Court set aside laws that unfairly discriminated between the sexes. For example, in *Craig v. Boren* (1976), the Court overturned an Oklahoma law that established different legal drinking ages for males and females. Other laws applying separate standards for men and women in alimony payments after divorce, jury service exemptions, and payments

☆ ═══════ ☆

*The "100-mile walk for equality" in 1976 protested against the
twelve angry men—the committee on privileges and elections in the
Virginia House of Representatives—who successfully blocked the
ratification of the ERA amendment by stalling it in committee.*

for worker's compensation and Social Security were also struck
down. Decisions such as these led to a further decline in support for the amendment.

Congress was flooded with proposals for an amendment to force
the government to balance the budget, to spend no more than it
received. The last time the federal government took in more
money than it spent was 1969. Since then, the government has
constantly had to borrow money to meet its expenses, and its
debt continued to grow. In the 1980s and in 1990, Congress
failed to muster the two-thirds majority needed to present such
an amendment to the states. (Opponents argued that it would
deny government the flexibility to deal with changes in the
economy.) Meanwhile, in 1985, Congress passed the Gramm-
Rudman-Hollings law, which established procedures to auto-
matically cut the budget and get it to balance. The Supreme
Court, however, rejected these procedures a year later. In 1995,
Congress was determined to make deep cuts in federal spending

programs. In this way, lawmakers hoped to balance the budget, reduce the government's debts, and give Americans a tax cut.

During the 1970s, more than 120 proposals were presented in Congress to limit the number of terms lawmakers could serve, the result of a number of scandals involving members of Congress. No action was taken. Meanwhile, the public was losing faith in Congress. Some argued that members of Congress stayed in office for so many years that they lost touch with the people back home who elected them. Given the advantages of office, members of Congress also easily defeated their challengers at election time. In recent years, newcomers made up less than 10 percent of Congress. To correct this situation, from 1992 to 1995, term limits for members of Congress were enacted in twenty-three states. In June 1995, the Supreme Court invalidated these measures, however, stating that a constitutional amendment was required. By March 29, 1995, four such proposals were defeated in the House of Representatives. Opponents argued that a term limits amendment would unfairly restrict voters' choices and deny the nation the experienced legislators it needed to handle its problems. Whether or not a new amendment is passed, some lawmakers have already volunteered to retire after serving several terms in office.

INFORMAL METHODS OF CHANGING THE CONSTITUTION

Just because amendments are defeated does not necessarily mean that the reforms they recommended will not eventually take place in a less formal manner. (Child labor, for example, was restricted without an adjustment to the Constitution.) Many modifications in the framers' outline for a federal government have been made by custom, by congressional law, by presidential practice, and by Supreme Court decision. These methods have proven just as long-lasting and effective as changes formally written into the Constitution.

By custom, political parties have simplified the choices voters must make on Election Day by narrowing the field of candidates and offering alternative programs. Nowhere are parties mentioned in the Constitution. They arose spontaneously when members of George Washington's government disagreed over policies. Secretary of State Thomas Jefferson favored plans to promote agriculture, while Secretary of the Treasury Alexander Hamilton preferred manufacturing and commercial development. Jefferson's supporters became known as the Democratic-Republicans, while Hamilton's followers were called the Federalists. These two groups began to contest elections, creating a two-party system in the United States.

In addition to its role in the amending process, Congress has also modified the Constitution by passing laws. The Constitution even encouraged Congress to do this. For example, the framers established a Supreme Court and then ordered Congress to create the rest of the federal court system. The lawmakers crafted a series of trial courts and courts of appeals. After listing the powers Congress could properly exercise, the framers also gave the legislature the right to do whatever was "necessary and proper" to carry out those powers. The "necessary and proper" clause in the Constitution gives Congress the ability to adapt to changing circumstances. Thus, the legislature used its power to "promote science and useful arts" and set up the National Aeronautics and Space Administration, which sent Americans to the moon. The space program was certainly not a development the framers could have foreseen when they wrote the Constitution!

Presidents have also altered the government created by the framers. When George Washington became president, he began to consult with the heads of government departments on a regular basis, thereby creating the cabinet. This advisory body cannot be found in the Constitution. The framers also never considered who would run the government when the president traveled abroad. When Woodrow Wilson became the first president to leave the country, he gave his vice president the power to conduct cabinet meetings. The Constitution gives vice presidents only the duty of presiding over the Senate and breaking tie votes. Modern presidents, however, have sent their vice presidents on diplomatic missions and put them in charge of various government commissions investigating national problems. These are just some of the ways presidents have modified the Constitution.

The Supreme Court's interpretations of the Constitution and its amendments have adapted the document to changing times. The framers, however, never said that the Court should make itself the guardian of the Constitution. Nevertheless, the Court assumed this power in 1803 in the case *Marbury v. Madison*, when it declared that an act of Congress violated the Constitution. To decide the case, the justices had to determine what the words of the Constitution meant and what the framers had intended. The Court has been interpreting the Constitution ever since. For example, after the Fourteenth Amendment was ratified, the United States started to become a major industrial nation. The Court began to use the amendment to protect newly formed corporations from state regulation rather than to help blacks claim their civil rights. Later, the justices reinterpreted the meaning of the amendment's phrases to benefit women and minorities.

☆ ☆ ☆

Americans are fortunate to have a system of government that provides both stability and flexibility. While the people of many other nations have had to repeatedly discard and replace their constitutions as new situations arose, Americans have been able to adapt theirs to changing circumstances. Amendments, customs, presidential practices, congressional laws, and Supreme Court decisions have kept the Constitution up to date. Yet the basic structure of American government still follows the framers' plan.

absentee ballots pieces of paper listing the candidates for office. They are mailed to voters who are temporarily absent from their home state or are ill. These voters must notify state officials in advance that they will be unable to vote on Election Day.

amendments formal changes in a legal document such as a law or the Constitution. For an amendment to be added to the Constitution, two-thirds of each house of Congress must agree to suggest the change, or Congress must call a convention to consider the change at the request of two-thirds of the state legislatures. Three-fourths of the state legislatures, or conventions in three-fourths of the states, must accept for ratification. There are now twenty-seven amendments to the Constitution.

bail money pledged to ensure that a person accused of a crime will show up for trial.

Bill of Rights guarantees of specific freedoms. The national Bill of Rights consists of the first ten amendments to the Constitution.

bills of attainder legislative punishments given to individuals or groups without first trying those parties in a court of law.

cabinet heads of government departments and other officials of the executive branch who give advice to the president.

common law a body of British law developed from custom and from the individual decisions of judges.

Congress the nation's lawmakers, divided into a House of Representatives, based on the population of each state, and a Senate, with two members for each state.

Constitution the framework that established the national government, defined and limited its powers, and outlined its relations with the states.

double jeopardy the Fifth Amendment protection from being tried twice for the same crime.

due process the Fifth Amendment requirement that proper and fair legal procedures must be followed before people accused of major crimes can be compelled to lose their lives, freedom, or property.

electors people in each state who are chosen to formally elect the president.

eminent domain   the seizure of private property by the government for a public use, such as highway construction. According to the Fifth Amendment, property owners must be paid a fair price when the government takes over their land.

ex post facto laws   laws that punish people for actions that were not illegal at the time the actions were taken.

fine   money paid as a penalty.

grand jury   from twelve to twenty-three people who decide whether there is sufficient evidence to charge a person with a crime so that he or she may be brought to trial.

judiciary   a court system that decides disputes over laws and judges those who break those laws.

legislature   an assembly of lawmakers at the national or state level.

perjury   telling a lie after having been sworn to tell the truth.

police powers   a state's authority to pass measures affecting the health, safety, and welfare of its citizens.

political parties   organizations that sponsor candidates for public office and help them get elected.

poll taxes   taxes used to prove that colonial and revolutionary voters were financially independent and responsible citizens. After the Civil War, Southern officials used such taxes to keep blacks and poor whites from voting.

president   the chief executive of the nation, responsible for carrying out the nation's laws.

primaries   nominating elections held by a political party in which voters can express their preferences for a particular candidate.

ratification   formal approval; in the case of amendments to the Constitution, the consent of three-fourths of the states is required.

self-incrimination   being compelled to testify against oneself in court. This is prohibited by the Fifth Amendment.

Supreme Court   the highest court in the United States.

teller vote   a vote in which members of Congress walk down the aisles to be counted for or against an issue, but actual names are not recorded.

writs of assistance   general and unlimited search warrants used and abused by the British to seek out smugglers in the colonies.

Anderson, Thornton. *Creating the Constitution: The Convention of 1787 and the First Congress.* University Park, Penn.: The Pennsylvania State University Press, 1993.

"Articles of Confederation," *The Federalist.* New York: The Modern Library, n.d.

Bernstein, Richard B., and Jerome Agel. *Amending America.* New York: Random House, 1993.

Christman, Margaret C. S. *The First Federal Congress 1789–1791.* Washington, D.C.: Smithsonian Institution Press, 1989.

Evans, Sara M. *Born for Liberty: A History of Women in America.* New York: Free Press, 1989.

Federalist, The. New York: Modern Library, n.d.

Feerick, John D. *The Twenty-fifth Amendment: Its Complete History and Applications.* New York: Fordham University Press, 1992.

Foner, Eric. *Reconstruction: America's Unfinished Revolution 1863–1877.* New York: Harper & Row, 1989.

——— and John A. Garraty, eds. *The Reader's Companion to American History.* Boston: Houghton Mifflin, 1991.

Gerberg, Mort. *The U.S. Constitution for Everyone.* New York: Perigee Books, 1987.

Glasser, Ira. *Visions of Liberty: The Bill of Rights for All Americans.* New York: Little, Brown, 1991.

Grimes, Alan P. *Democracy and the Amendments to the Constitution.* Lanham, Md.: University Press of America, 1987.

Hall, Kermit L., ed. *The Oxford Companion to the Supreme Court.* New York: Oxford University Press, 1992.

Ketcham, Ralph, ed. *The Anti-Federalist Papers and the Constitutional Convention Debates.* New York: Mentor Books, 1986.

Konvitz, Milton R. "The Bill of Rights: Amendments I–X," *An American Primer,* Daniel J. Boorstin, ed. New York: Meridian Books, 1985.

Kurland, Philip B. "Article V and the Amending Process," *An American Primer,* Daniel J. Boorstin, ed. New York: Meridian Books, 1985.

Rutland, Robert A. *The Birth of the Bill of Rights 1776–1791.* Boston: Northeastern University Press, 1983.

Schlesinger, Arthur M., Jr. "The Future of the Vice Presidency," *The Cycles of American History.* Boston: Houghton Mifflin, 1986.

Trussell, C. P. "Democrats Fight Third-Term Curb," *New York Times*, March 11, 1947, p. 1.

Wise, James W., ed. *Our Bill of Rights: What It Means to Me.* New York: Bill of Rights Sesquicentenntial Committee, 1941.

Brill, Marlene Targ. *Let Women Vote!* Brookfield, Conn.: Millbrook, 1995.

Cohen, Daniel. *Prohibition: America Makes Alcohol Illegal.* Brookfield, Conn.: Millbrook, 1995.

Coleman, Warren. *The Bill of Rights.* Chicago: Childrens Press, 1987.

Hauptly, Denis J. *A Convention of Delegates: The Creation of the Constitution.* New York: Atheneum, 1987.

League of Women Voters. *From Ordinance to Constitution: Government of and by the People.* Cleveland: League of Women Voters of Cleveland Educational Fund, 1987.

Lindop, Edmund. *Birth of the Constitution.* Springfield, N.J.: Enslow, 1987.

McPhillips, Martin. *The Constitutional Convention.* Parsippany, N.J.: Silver-Burdett, 1985.

Meltzer, Milton. *The Bill of Rights: How We Got It and What It Means.* New York: Crowell Junior Books, 1990.

Stein, Conrad. *The Bill of Rights.* Chicago: Childrens Press, 1992.

———. *The Story of the Nineteenth Amendment.* Chicago: Childrens Press, 1982.

INDEX